IMAGES
of America

CITY ISLAND
AND
ORCHARD BEACH

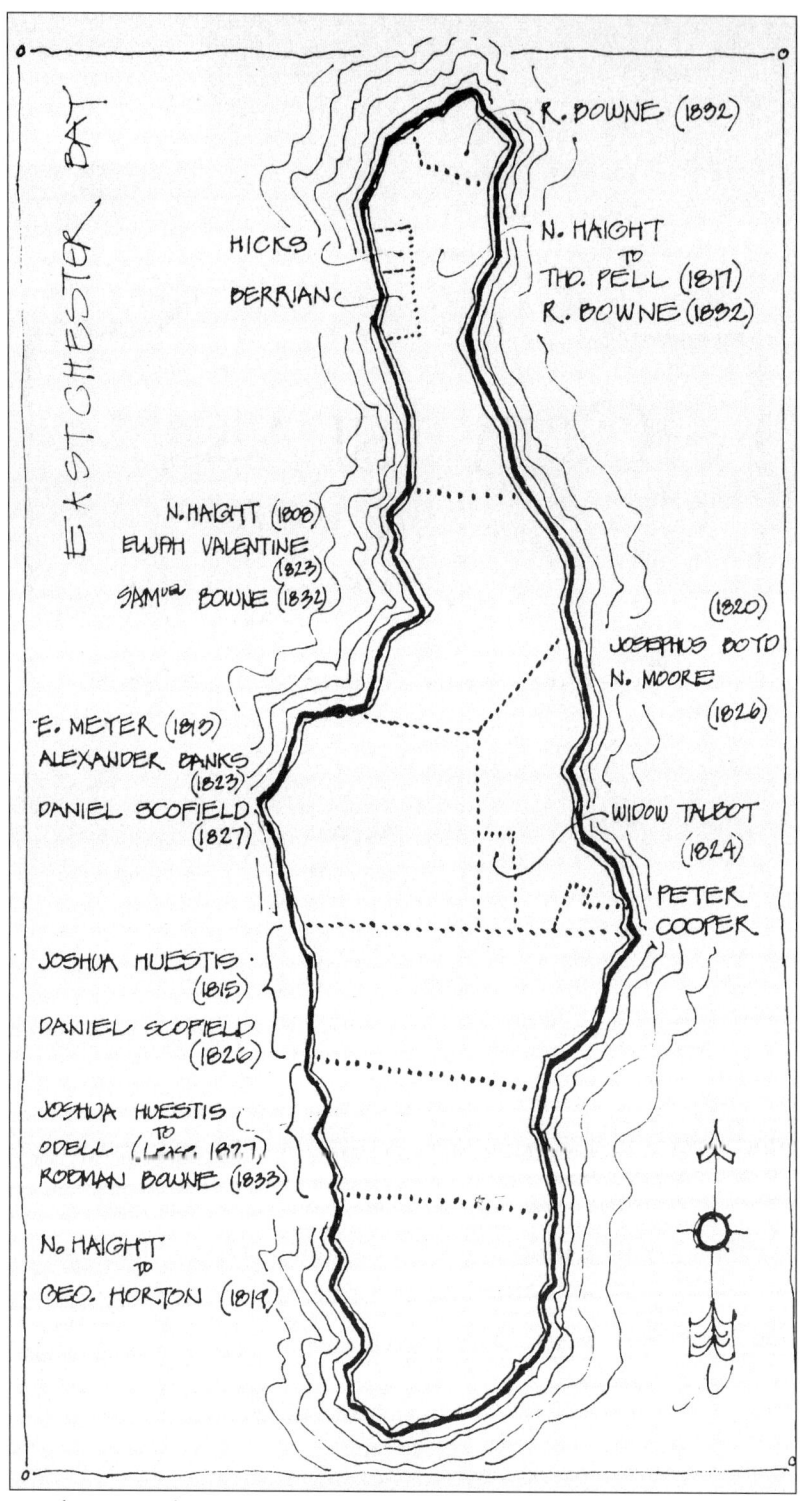

This line map drawing indicates the major landowners on City Island prior to 1836. (Courtesy of the Westchester County Historical Society.)

IMAGES
of America

CITY ISLAND
AND
ORCHARD BEACH

Catherine A. Scott

ARCADIA

Published by Arcadia Publishing,
an imprint of Tempus Publishing, Inc.
2 Cumberland Street
Charleston, SC 29401

Printed in Great Britain.

Library of Congress Catalog Card Number: Applied for.

For all general information contact Arcadia Publishing at:
Telephone 843-853-2070
Fax 843-853-0044
E-Mail edit@arcadiaimages.com

For customer service and orders:
Toll-Free 1-888-313-BOOK

Visit us on the internet at http://www.arcadiaimages.com

Real estate agent Joseph P. Day published a map in 1915 advertising real estate on City Island that focused on the island's many healthful parks. A close look shows that Rodman Park, Bartow Park, Sound Park, Palmer Park, and Minneford Park were situated on the island at that time. High Island can be seen at the northern tip of City Island.

CONTENTS

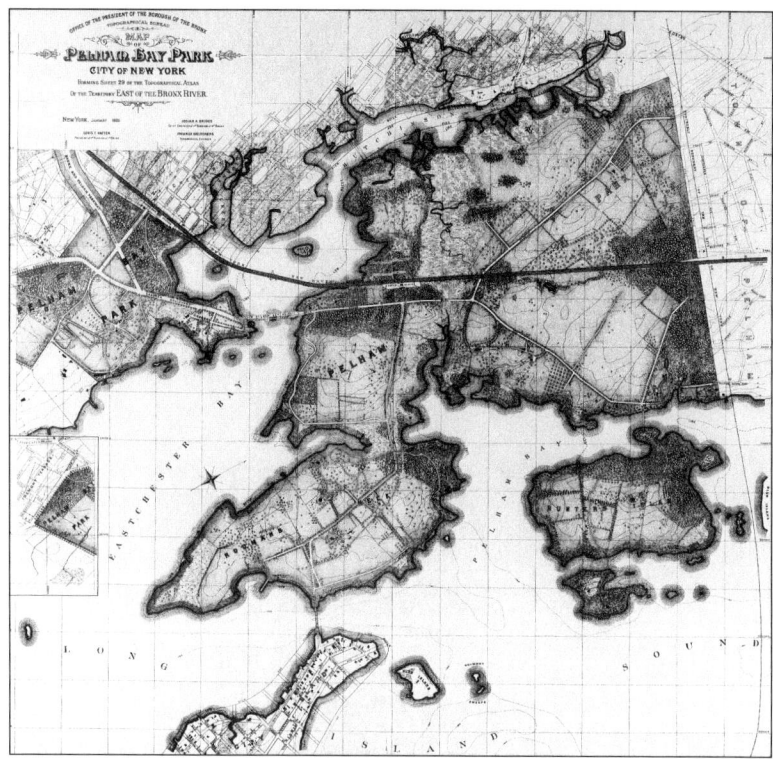

This 1906 topographical map of the northern tip of City Island (lower left) and its environs shows the area before the city built Orchard Beach in 1935, and before its parking lot connected Hunter and Twin Islands (lower right) to the mainland of Rodman's Neck (the land above City Island).

ACKNOWLEDGMENTS

This book would not have been possible without the invaluable assistance of Tom Nye of the City Island Historical Museum, whose patience, generosity, and knowledge contributed to its content. Mr. Nye supplied the majority of photographs from the museum as well as from his personal collection. I wish to also thank those who over the years graciously donated family photos to the museum for all to enjoy.

I appreciate the loan of pictures from the following people: Connie and Hy Cantor, William Clancy, Al DeAngelo, Natalie and Gus Gallowitz, Diane and Alan Henshaw, Peter LaScala, William and Netta McDaniel, Karen Nani of the *Island Current*, Sister James Patrick, the New York City Department of Parks & Recreation, Russell Rasmussen, Tyler Rhodes, Jorge Santiago, and Howard Smith. I am deeply grateful to John Collazzi, Rick DeWitt, and Vincent Hecker for providing the technical help necessary to put together this photographic history of City Island.

—C.S.

INTRODUCTION

City Island resounds in the hearts of its residents. Initially known as Minnewits, Great Minneford, or Minnefers (after local Native Americans), it was named "City Island" following an unsuccessful development plan by Benjamin Palmer to build a city around a seaport. The island's theme song, "City Island, Star of the Sea," written long ago by Jeanne Walsh, describes the sentiments of those living on the tiny one-mile-long-by-one-mile-wide island. Lying between Long Island Sound and Eastchester Bay, City Island indeed shines brightly as the "Star of the Sea" in Bronx County, New York City.

The story of City Island and Tent City/Orchard Beach in Pelham Bay Park really begins at the end of the Lenape American Indian era along the East Coast of the United States. European colonists arriving in increasing numbers in the 1600s forced Native-American tribes in the vicinity to sell or abandon their lands and resettle to upper New York State, New Jersey, or Pennsylvania to avoid further confrontation.

City Island became inhabited during the earliest Colonial days as part of the First Discovery, in which England claimed portions of North America. This is evidenced by a Westchester County conveyance in 1685, listing several houses, barns, and other buildings on the island. King Charles granted his brother James, Duke of York, huge tracts of land in 1664 including New York. The duke authorized Colonel Richard Nicolls to manage these lands; Colonel Nicolls, in turn, issued a grant to Thomas Pell, beginning a reign of Pell family ownership over land in Westchester County and the town of Pelham, which City Island and Pelham Bay Park were part of at that time. This reign lasted until 1749, when ownership of City Island passed from the Pell family to others such as Amos Dodge and Samuel Rodman.

History unfolds in the first chapter with the significant role the area played in the Revolutionary War. After the war, Europeans settled here, as the lure of the sea and healthy air set a natural stage for related activities. Early industries prospered only to disappear, such as the successful oyster business in the early 1800s that slowly died following the turn of the century. The clay and pottery enterprise and salt extraction plant that removed salt from evaporated sea water both played an important part in City Island's past. Long gone are the experienced Hellgate Pilots who guided vessels safely from the south end of City Island to Manhattan through the treacherous twisted channel of the East River's Hellgate.

Slow urbanization continued after the Revolutionary War, when land owners Joshua Hustis and Nicholas Haight laid out a road in 1811 on City Island. At that time, City Island and the

Orchard Beach area fell under the jurisdiction of the Town of Pelham in Westchester County. A toll bridge, erected in 1873 connecting City Island to the mainland, marked an important step in advancing City Island's growth. Stagecoaches, horse cars, and a monorail, although not totally reliable, offered far superior modes of transportation than did ferries.

The ensuing chapters describe the growth of the City Island community, its people, services, industries, and transportation. The need arose for houses of worship, schools, retailers, and government services. Magnificent hotels, bathing clubs, and the finest New York City restaurants gradually dotted the island. Another perspective visually presented brings to light how residents spent their leisure time—from volunteering in organizations and clubs, to participating in sports and recreation. The book explains how "Tent City," a summer bungalow colony established in the late 1890s, evolved into Orchard Beach, New York City's showcase swimming and recreation area.

Without a doubt, however, shipbuilding rose as the premier industry on City Island, with craftsmen and engineers creating magnificent yachts, world-class racing boats, and America's Cup winners. Shipbuilders and sailmakers found the island an ideal place because of its deep water, good anchorage, easy access to Manhattan, and seafaring population. Millionaires such as Sir Thomas Lipton commissioned their luxury yachts in the early 1900s at the island's well-known shipyards. City Island was known throughout the country for its boat designs and unique craftsmanship.

During World War I and II, the government authorized shipyards to build mine sweepers, torpedo boats, tugboats, and landing craft. Following World War II, the grand era of shipbuilding and hotels gradually diminished. Shipyards built smaller boats more in demand than large yachts costing huge amounts of money to design and maintain. The heyday for luxury boating was over. Fiberglass boats replaced the wooden vessels that were the yards' specialty. But the island remained a vibrant community, meeting changing needs and technology. Shipyards gave way to marinas that repaired and berthed smaller vessels, an industry that continues today.

The "Star of the Sea" remains a community known throughout New York City for its fine seafood restaurants, yacht clubs, antique stores, art galleries, fishing boats, and boat rental businesses. The renovated Orchard Beach, once a location of tents and bungalows, is today an outstanding recreation facility attracting thousands of tourists each season. The intent of the author is to delight readers by offering them a chance to trace the well-researched fascinating history of City Island and Orchard Beach.

This sign, prominently displayed at top of the City Island Bridge, welcomes residents and visitors to the island.

One

THE EARLY VILLAGE, FIRST FAMILIES, AND ECONOMY

The Horton family at the turn of the century operated a refreshment stand at Beldon Point Pier, the south end of City Island. George Washington Horton purchased the southern part of the island in 1819 from Joshua Hustis and settled his family here. In 1853 Moses Bell, a potter from Garrison, New York, found blue clay on Mr. Horton's property and established a successful pottery business along the west shore between Marine and Pilot Streets.

Split Rock, shown here *c.* 1907 near the Bronx/Westchester County line, is believed to mark the camp site of Ann Hutchinson, who established one of the earliest known settlements near City Island. Ms. Hutchinson and her followers arrived near Split Rock in 1642 after leaving New England to seek religious freedom. Ann and her colony, except for one girl, were murdered in a Native-American attack. The Hutchinson River Parkway and Hutchinson River are named after the courageous leader.

E.C. Cooper built a small solar salt plant in 1830 along Banta Lane and east Carroll Street. This was probably the first commercial enterprise on the island. The sun's rays evaporated seawater and deposited salt crystals, using inclined plane beds for salt rooms and a windmill to raise the water. This etching, from the 1836 *Journal of the American Institute*, is the earliest known extant illustration of City Island. The business closed because salt mining become more economical in other parts of the country.

Glover's Rock, c. 1907, is located in Pelham Bay Park on Orchard Beach Road near City Island. The plaque commemorates the Battle of Pell's Point, which took place on October 18, 1776. Colonel John Glover and 750 soldiers fought 4,000 British and Hession troops, thus delaying the British long enough for General George Washington and his exhausted troops to safely reach White Plains and regroup. Benjamin Palmer, who purchased City Island in 1761, supported the rebellious Americans. As a result, the British killed his cattle, burned his possessions, and imprisoned his family. The British regularly attacked City Island, whose residents for the most part sympathized with the American cause.

Vera Horton (left) and her playmates stand near the Belden Point Pier in 1901. Statistics from 1854 reveal that three farms existed on City Island, operated by George W. Horton, William Schofield, and David Schofield. Belden Point is named after William Belden, who purchased the south end in 1885 from Stephen Decator Horton, a descendant of G.W. Horton. Mr. Belden wanted to build a casino and amusement park, plans that never materialized.

Shipping News Office and Information Bureau, City Island, N. Y.

S.D Horton Jr. built an observatory at the Shipping News Office, located at 88 City Island Avenue on the corner of Marine Street, for the Maritime Association of New York, Western Union, and the U.S. Signal Service. In 1910 the building doubled as a quarantine station, with Dr. N. Horton as its health officer. Vessels could not proceed to New York City unless passengers received a clean bill of health. Occupying the house in later years were the Upper Bronx Community Center and, in 1936, the Marine Restaurant. The building is shown here in the early 1900s.

Vera Horton and her family sit in their new car on the City Island pier at Belden Point and Long Island Sound, c. 1900. When autos first became popular in the late 1800s and early 1900s, only the wealthy could afford this luxury. Notice the oyster sloop in the background, another of City Island's early successful businesses that eventually died.

THE PIER, CITY ISLAND, N. Y.

The Belden Point Pier, located at the south end of City Island, is shown here in the early 1900s. The *Mary Starr* is docked at the end of the pier, which was a popular spot for residents and visitors to fish and take boat rides. The deteriorated structure was demolished in the 1950s.

This photograph of City Island Avenue was taken looking north from the Belden Point Pier in the early 1900s. Johnny's Reef Restaurant is now situated on the right looking north and Duryea's Restaurant is on the left. In the 1800s Belden Point boasted large estates and elitist resorts. After the turn of the century, the property was broken down into smaller tracts and developed as a summer resort for the middle class, featuring picnic tables, bathhouses, and pavilions.

13

No. 8.—Camp St. Bartholomew Club, Belden Point, City Island, N. Y.

At the turn of the century, a large picnic grove was set up on the southeast section of Belden Point. St. Bartholemew's Church of New York established a non-sectarian club facing Eastchester Bay for men in this area. Club members lived in tents during the summer months. The church provided meals in a large mess tent.

The Hellgate Pilot House, at the Consolidated Boat Yard on Pilot Street, faces Long Island Sound. The house stands today as a reminder of when City Island became the home of the Hellgate Pilots Association, located at the Shipping News Office on the corner of City Island Avenue and Marine Street. Many City Island men worked as Hellgate Pilots, an important job from the mid-1800s until 1967. Men stood in the house watching for ships traveling to Manhattan. Pilots guided the vessels to their destination through treacherous Hellgate waters.

The Hellgate Bridge, which made a physical connection with the Long Island and Pennsylvania Railroad system, is shown here under construction (in 1915, above) and in its completed state (in 1919, below). Hellgate is the back door to the port of New York and forms the channel of the East River where Long Island Sound and the East River converge. It is a dangerous waterway, with fierce tides, cross currents, jagged rocks, whirlpools, and a narrow, twisted channel near 95th Street. Hellgate pilots were instituted through an Act of Legislature in 1847. Pilots boarded steamboats, ocean freighters, coal schooners, etc, from City Island's north end and guided them to New York. The Sandy Hook Pilots Assoc. absorbed the Hellgate Pilots in 1967, thus ending a City Island legacy. The first pilots were J. Fordham, the Hortons, D. Pell, the Schofields, N. Abbott, and G. Stevens.

Hell Gate Bridge and East River, New York City.

Copyright 1916 by Irving Underhill, N. Y.

This iceboat was built by island resident Fred Glasier in the early 1900s. Mr. Glasier often raced other iceboat owners, a popular winter sport on the frozen waters surrounding City Island.

Owners and their iceboats line up along Eastchester Bay at the turn of the century, preparing to engage in an iceboat race. Many of the boats were handmade by the owners; some of the boats pictured here are the *Goldust Bowl*, the *Scooter*, and the *Syndicate*.

The *Petrol*, a 32-foot oyster sloop, was built by Fred Glasier of Fordham Street in 1896. The smaller skiff trailing the sloop gathered oysters from shallow waters. Part of the *Petrol*'s hull is displayed in the City Island Historical Museum. Oyster sloops dominated City Island's boat building industry in the early 1800s. The largest steam-powered oyster dredge in the country was the 77-foot, 91-ton *Joshua Leviness*, built in 1876 on City Island.

City Island oystermen gather along the western shore of City Island, between Fordham and Bay Streets, in 1910. Oystering became a prime source of income for many City Island settlers. In 1830 Orrin Fordham developed America's first oyster cultivation business by propagating oysters from seed caught upon artificial beds or prepared receptacles.

William Hoffman (left) poses with his baby sister Dorothy on City Island at the turn of the century. Their father, William Sr., made his living as an oysterman. He owned an oyster skiff that delivered oysters to barges for workers to clean and prepare for shipping to various ports. By the early 1890s, the bulk of the prosperous oystering business ceased due to various factors. Oysters faced destruction by sea stars and borers, off-shore thieves, over-harvesting of the beds in Eastchester Bay, and the pollution of local waters. The ongoing disputes between the Oystermen's Protective Association and private oyster dredging companies also created economic hardships.

An oyster barge sits in the waters of Eastchester Bay between Bay and Fordham Streets in the early 1900s. The people in the rowboat are preparing to clean and shuck oysters in the well of the barge. In 1888, island residents Bergen and Bowden became dealers and shippers of oysters, hiring men to open almost 50,000 oysters each day for shipments to Buffalo and Chicago. Men worked by the piece, earning $3 to $5.50 daily.

The schooner *Samuel S. Thorpe*, shown here in the early 1900s, was built in 1880 at David Carll's shipyard on City Island. The 160-foot three-masted schooner was owned by the Bailey family and was used commercially in England and the South Pacific until the 1920s. In 1862, David Carll opened a shipyard, the first on City Island, at east Pilot Street. Mr. Carll built many well-known schooner yachts, thus paving the way for other successful shipyards to follow.

Charles Harold and his family pose at their home on Centre Street in 1914. Mr. Harold, a boatbuilder, worked as superintendent of City Island's famous Nevins Shipyard at the time.

Angie and Charles Glasier stand in front of their home at 8 Fordham Street, which is now known as 80 Fordham Street, *c.* 1888. Their father, Frederick, was a seaman who built oyster sloops and other types of boats on City Island. The Glasier family purchased the Fordham Street house in 1886. The Pelham Westchester statistics of 1890 reveal that 1,206 people lived on City Island. The population of the island began to expand after a bridge was built in 1873 connecting it to the mainland.

The Black House, *c.* 1915, was located along Eastchester Bay and Pilot Street, and was built in 1896 by a lawyer who used it as a summer home. Residents thought the house was haunted because they heard eerie sounds and shrieks when the wind blew through the eight-sided structure. It was abandoned during World War I and torn down in the early 1930s. Pickwick Terrace, a six-story apartment building, now occupies the site.

This photograph of the McDaniel bungalow (in the forefront), located on west Marine Street, was taken c. 1920. The Black House (now the apartment building known as Pickwick Terrace) stands on the left at the end of west Pilot Street behind the bungalow. The City Island Yacht Club sits on the far right. The bungalow was used as a summer cottage by the Taylor family, which later sold it to William and Natalie McDaniel.

Carrie Glasier poses in front of 8 Fordham Street at around turn of the century. At that time, every house on City Island used a well to pump fresh water. Young girls Carrie's age kept themselves busy with schoolwork, housework, and gardening. Entertainment included social functions at the local church, swimming, gathering oysters, sleigh riding, races, embroidery, participating in games such as corn-bag popping and bursting soap bubbles, and playing musical instruments such as the piano or violin.

The McDaniel family gathered on Marine Street for a group photo in the early 1920s. William McDaniel owned and operated the *Arbus*, a boat that delivered fresh water and supplies to large ships laid up near City Island. The family owned the vessel from the turn of the century to the 1950s.

The Fordham family stands in front of 340 City Island Avenue, *c.* 1890s. Dr. Norbert Sander's medical building is now located here. Members of the Fordham family were among City Island's early settlers. In 1894 Orrin Fordham founded the first newspaper on the island, the *City Island Drift*. When Orrin married Emma Abbott in 1893, Mt. Vernon news accounts stated "the wedding ceremony was attended by City Island's elite."

The Francis Vail Estate on Paulis Place, between west Hawkins and Fordham Streets, is shown here in the early 1900s. The structure remains today as a reminder of City Island's past and present grand houses and English-style gardens. Prior to 1836, several people owned estates on City Island, including D. Schofield, E. Meyer, Alexander Banks, George Horton, Peter Cooper, E. Valentine, Samuel Bowne, Rodman Bowne, Nicholas Haight, and T. Pell.

In the early 1900s, the Francis Vail Estate gardens, along with many other gardens on City Island and in other areas of New York, were greatly influenced by the English, whose love of free-form flower beds, sumptuous borders, winding paths, luxurious trees, colorful flowers and vegetables, clipped topiary, and detail to character made distinctive and exquisite garden designs.

King Avenue is shown here in the early 1900s, before it was paved and fully developed. It is named after Elisha King, a wealthy statesman who owned nearby High Island. He purchased property along City Island's eastern shoreline in 1829 to obtain landing privileges to High Island. King Avenue extends to that landing place.

This is City Island Avenue and east Bay Street looking south in January 1906. On the left, not seen in the picture, was the Vickery Brothers stable and restaurant. Most of the buildings in the picture exist today.

In the early days, horse-drawn sleds, such as the one pictured here in 1918, traveled over frozen waters to unload cargo from large ships and deliver necessary goods to City Island residents.

City Island residents try to dig themselves out from a major snowfall in March 1906. Snow blowers had not been invented at that time, necessitating long hours of shoveling. High rubber boots and wool winter hats kept the cold at bay.

The brick Devil's Stepping Stones Lighthouse, shown here in the early 1900s, was built in 1877. It lies in Long Island Sound south of City Island, and marks the entrance of the East River to New York City. Lighthouses were vital to ensuring ships a safe voyage around dangerous waters. Legend claims the lighthouse was named after the Devil, who tried to deter Westchester County Indians from capturing him by throwing stones into the water as he was fleeing to Long Island. Still another legend says that Native Americans told the early Dutch and English settlers that an evil spirit used the nearby dangerous reefs as stepping stones to cross the sound to the Long Island shores. The lighthouse has a fixed green light and became automated in 1966.

Execution Lighthouse was built in 1867. It lies east of City Island in Long Island Sound and is fronted by a chain of dangerous rocky islands. One legend claims it was named for American Revolutionists who died here after the English tied them to the rocks, to be executed by the high tide. It became automated in 1979, and is shown here in the early 1900s.

Two

FOUNDATION OF A
COMMUNITY

The old 77th Police Precinct Station, pictured here in the early 1900s, was formerly City Island's second public school and is now the site of Hawkins Street Park. Orchard Street (on the left) was later renamed Hawkins Street. The front edifice of the building (not the porch) became part of a house currently on Centre Street. In 1907 the precinct boasted 16 policemen, 3 lieutenants, and 3 sergeants. The *Bronx Home News* reported that a state investigator criticized the police station for having two cells as "City Island is a very law abiding place, and the police never have any business except when the crowds go up from downtown and start something."

City Island's second schoolhouse, located in what is now Hawkins Street Park (on the corner of City Island Avenue and Hawkins Street), is shown here in the late 1800s. School authorities deemed the building unsafe for children, particularly if a fire ever occurred. An outside staircase was therefore built (visible on the left). After New York City annexed City Island, it built a new school building at 190 Fordham Street, and the structure on Hawkins Street was converted into a police station.

This painting of Grace Episcopal Church was done by City Island artist Harold Vandervoort Walsh. The church was organized in 1862 under the auspices of Christ Church in Pelham and the Bolton family. The Gothic-style structure was built at the corner of Pilot Street and City Island Avenue in 1865 on land donated by George W. Horton. The Rev. Cornelius Bolton of Christ Church rowed to City Island once a month to offer Sunday services. Carpenters from David Carll's shipyard helped build the church.

The 38th Sub-Precinct Police Station was located on the east side of Marine Street, on the corner of City Island Avenue, at turn of the century. From left to right are the following: (sitting) Ben Rolff and Bill Garner; (standing) Pat Grady, Bill Riley, Mr. Sisson, and L. Smith. This precinct became the 77th Police Precinct on January 1, 1908, when precincts were numbered. In 1893, Constable Frank Glazier arrested "Bob the Kisser," who kissed at least 10 unescorted females against their will. He was placed under $100 bail and everyone praised the City Island police officers.

This *c.* 1930s ceremony took place at Hawkins Street Park. The former building on the property, which had served as the second schoolhouse on City Island and later as a police station, was razed in the early 1930s to create Hawkins Park. After the city demolished the building, it built a police booth (upper left) that contained a phone for emergencies.

No. 1—Fire Department, City Island, N. Y.

After New York City annexed City Island, it purchased the property at 169 Schofield Street in 1898 and constructed a wood fire station there for paid workers. Harry Booth built the firehouse, shown here in 1908, at a cost of $8,000. The brick fire station currently on the site was erected in 1940. While the structure underwent renovations, the fire department moved into temporary headquarters on Minneford Lane, then to the corner of King Avenue and Fordham Street. Firefighters stored their trucks across the street from the Public School 17 building on Fordham Street. The Trinity Methodist Church bell served as City Island's official fire alarm.

Firefighters from the Minneford Engine House, a volunteer fire company on Fordham Street between William Avenue and City Island Avenue, pose *c.* 1900. This was one of three volunteer fire companies protecting City Island. The others were the Minneford Hose Company and the City Island Hook & Ladder. In 1893 the three companies acquired a steamer fire engine, nicknaming it the "Minneford." The men sponsored picnics to raise money for churches and other benefits.

Members of the City Island's Life Saving Corps pose for a photograph in 1908. From left to right are Mr. Schoeffer, E. Beam, N. Lee, four unidentified men and a small boy, Lester Bettigieu, Harry Lott, Ben May, Clarence Fordham, Oscar Fordham (with oar), Gus Jackob (with mustache), and John Bottger.

The Volunteer Life Saving Corps in 1900 consisted of the following people, from left to right: (bottom row) John Thompson and Harvey Hauptner; (middle row) Ed Hearle Jr.; (top row) Ed Hearle Sr., Vic Lane, Harry Carey, Len Hauptner, and Charles Stringham. The Life Saving Corps held annual water carnivals to demonstrate the skills and efficiency of its volunteers.

No. 5—Trinity M.E. Church, City Island, N.Y.

The Trinity United Methodist Church, shown here in 1907, was built in 1878 on the former site of the Non-Pareil Baseball Field at the corner of City Island Avenue and Bay Street. A parsonage on Bay Street adjoining the church was acquired later, and a connecting passageway was added in 1932. The church bell served as the official fire alarm for City Island. Five rapid strokes in succession indicated a fire in progress. After a short pause, the church's caretaker or his assistant struck the number of bells corresponding to the fire's location. For instance, one tap meant that portion of the island north of Ditmars Street, east and west, and so on.

Parade marchers celebrating the raising of the service flag pose in front of the Trinity United Methodist Church in 1918. The first Methodist church building was located on land donated by Joshua Leviness, south of the present Crab Shanty Restaurant at the corner of Tier Street and City Island Avenue. Its hall served as a center for community activities and entertainment.

Members of the Trinity United Methodist Church pose at the corner of Bay Street and City Island Avenue, c. 1918. From left to right are as follows: (bottom row) William Booth, Gordon Ward, William Attrill, Sam Booth, and Mrs. Sumner; (top row) Dr. George Reynolds, John O. Fordham, unidentified, and Rev. Harris Smith.

33

City Island's first one-room schoolhouse, shown here c. 1860s, opened in 1839 on the site of the current playground of Public School 175 on City Island Avenue. In 1838, the Town of Pelham formed City Island School District No. 2 and built the first schoolhouse. The school board raised money through assessments to cover various expenses, such as yearly fuel. In 1847, the school was enlarged and a new teacher, Mary Tooker, was hired. In the early days, classes were held in the home of Rachel S. Fordham.

City Island schoolchildren pose in front of the public school on Flag Raising Day, c. 1900. A second school was built in the 1860s at the corner of Hawkins Street and City Island Avenue. The school operated until 1898, when the City of New York built a modern structure at 190 Fordham Street, the site of the island's first cemetery.

City Island Public School No. 17.

Public School 17 was located at 190 Fordham Street. Shown here in the early 1930s, it was built in 1897 after New York City annexed City Island. The building was extended in 1930 and remained the only school on the island until the Catholic Church built St. Mary Star of the Sea School on Minneford Avenue. Public School 175, erected on City Island Avenue, replaced this building in the late 1970s. The old structure on Fordham Street was later converted to condominium units housing the City Island Community Center and Nautical Museum.

Public School 17 students pose for camera, c. 1928. The old schoolyard, where hundreds of children played tag and ball, now accommodates parking for vehicles owned by residents of the condominium units.

This eighth grade graduating class photo was taken in the schoolyard of Public School 17 at 190 Fordham Street in the early 1930s. Miss May Mulligan (middle row, flowered dress) was a popular eighth grade teacher. Standing on her left is principal Mary Fitzpatrick.

Rev. James A. Kilroe (seated left) was the pastor of St. Mary Star of the Sea Church in 1935, when this graduation day photo was taken. The parish built a new community hall attached to what is now the convent, which in the early 1900s faced Minneford Avenue. The first parochial school was established in 1926 on Minneford Avenue, with classes held in this community hall. In 1931, the school opened for small kindergarten through fifth grade classes. It gradually accommodated the full eight grades.

St. Mary Star of the Sea Church is shown here in the early 1900s. Property was purchased at the present St. Mary's Church location on City Island Avenue, and a Mission Chapel erected in 1886. The wooden chapel burned in 1890 but parishioners raised money and quickly built a church in its place the following year. Another fire destroyed the structure in 1956, but once again St. Mary's church and rectory were rebuilt, this time in 1959, at the same site.

This St. Mary Star of the Sea Church, pictured here before it burned down in 1956, was completed in 1891. Catholic Church services began on City Island in 1878, when City Island and Hart Island became the 11th mission of St. Raymond's Church, the mother church of the Bronx. The first mission was held at the Hotel Ben Hur, situated at the parking lot of Bridge Boat Sales on Bridge Street. Before the church was built, masses were held in the private homes of parishioners.

This graduation day photograph was taken at St. Mary Star of the Sea School in 1945. Rev. Edward C. Nilan headed St. Mary Star of the Sea Church (seated middle) for the next 23 years. The parish built a new school in 1948 as enrollment climbed from 30 to 200 in 1945. The convent, originally located on the school site, moved to Kilroe Street, and a new wing was added to allow for additional living quarters. The Dominican Sisters of Blauvelt continue to teach students at the school.

In the early 1950s, this confirmation day was held at the schoolyard of St. Mary Star of the Sea School, facing Long Island Sound. In 1992 a violent northeast storm hit City Island and severely damaged the schoolyard and the house seen here across the street.

Members of Temple Beth-El received an award from the United Jewish Appeal in 1967. Sam Bierman (fourth from left), who owned a pharmacy on City Island, was one of 17 founding members in 1934 and was regarded as a great civic leader. Families initially met in private homes with services held at the American Legion, the Trinity Methodist Church hall, and the Grace Episcopal Church hall. The congregation dedicated the temple building in 1957 at 480 City Island Avenue, where it remains a sanctuary for worship.

Connie Cantor and her Hebrew kindergarten class pose at Temple Beth-El in 1964. The Temple organized a Jewish religious school on City Island in 1942, with classes held in the Trinity Methodist Church hall. The Temple continues as a center for Jewish education.

The Vickery Brothers Grocery Store, c. 1900, eventually became the site of the City Island Library at East Bay Street and City Island Avenue. The library was formed in 1911 by a committee directed by H.C. Appleton and Mrs. Robert Jacob, wife of a local shipyard owner, who stocked the library with their personal books. It later moved to Buckbinder's drugstore near Cross Street, and then to 325 City Island Avenue. In 1971 the library opened at its present site. Several years ago the city expanded the building.

The City Island Post Office, c. 1940s, was located at the corner of City Island Avenue and Tier Street, where the Crab Shanty Restaurant now stands. Horse riders and stagecoaches delivered mail in Colonial days along Boston Post Road from New England, and by oyster sloop from New York City. In 1862, a post office at Bartow Station serviced the island. A post office was set up in 1896 in Waterhouse's grocery store on Fordham Place. Later, the facility was temporarily housed at 329 City Island Avenue.

Three

TRANSPORTATION MARKS THE ISLAND'S GROWTH

Residents rejoiced when trolley car service was installed to City Island in 1914. Area officials, dignitaries, and residents gathered on the first day of trolley car service to City Island on August 3, 1914. Gone were the days of horse cars and the unreliable monorail. The 36-foot-long electric trolley cars were self-propelled by electricity from storage batteries. They ran from Bartow Station to Belden Point for a 5¢ fare. Trolley cars remained the principal means of transportation until the city government introduced buses.

Before the City Island Bridge was built, traveling to and from City Island could only be achieved by ferry or boat. This photograph shows the old wooden City Island Bridge at the turn of the century. Before the bridge, two ferries operated—one from the north end of the island to Rodman's Neck, and another from the south end to Port Washington in Long Island. A 3¢ wooden toll bridge was finally erected in 1873 through the efforts of G.W. Horton, S.D. Horton, David Carll, Joshua Leviness, and Benjamin Hegemen, who formed a stock company in 1868 for this purpose.

The old City Island Bridge spanned 1,000 feet from the west end of Bridge Street to the mainland and featured a 120-foot draw. It was purportedly built with materials from the *North Carolina*, an old U.S. battleship dismantled at Carll's Shipyard in City Island. New York City removed the toll in 1895 when it acquired City Island from Westchester County. In 1901 a steel bridge next to the old wooden bridge was built. It cost $250,000 and opened on a turntable basis.

East Entrance City Island Bridge. N Y.

A couple travels to City Island over the City Island Bridge in a horse and buggy, *c.* 1908. The Vickery Brothers horse-drawn livery service traveled off the island, as seen at left. In 1873 Robert Vickery operated the stagecoach, the forerunner of horse cars. It ran from City Island to Mt. Vernon prior to the establishment of Bartow Station.

Bartow and City Island street car line.

The Age of Progress arrived when horse cars replaced the earlier stagecoach line on City Island about 1887. This picture dates from the early 1900s. The horse car ran on tracks and connected with trains at Bartow Station. Initially they brought travelers to the Marshall Mansion (Colonial Inn), at the park side of the City Island Bridge, where livery service was available. Tracks were later placed along City Island Avenue to the Grace Episcopal Church on Pilot Street.

New York City decided to improve transportation services for City Island by establishing a monorail in 1910. The 50-foot cars, using two overhead rails and a single track, were driven by two separate alternating motors. The four wheels ran on a single rail spiked to ties. Above the cars at each end were flexible arms connected with an X-shaped truck and two L-shaped overhead guide rails that conducted electricity.

Monorail Road ran from Bartow Station to the City Island Bridge, 1910. After exiting the monorail at the bridge, people boarded a horse car to City Island. The monorail fare was 10¢.

One of the Weaver Brothers stands next to his stagecoach, *c.* late 1800s. The brothers owned a grocery store on City Island Avenue, and used their coach to deliver goods to City Island residents.

City Island Horse Car, City Island, New York

Horses Bob and Harry, shown here in the early 1900s, pulled the Pelham Park and City Island horse cars thousands of times. The horses were on the job for 16 years along with their driver, Patrick Burns of Pell Street. A pot-bellied stove inside the car provided heat for passengers during the winter months.

Workers on the horse car line up pose for a picture in 1908. Those identified are Alec Jackson (standing on the left) and Ernest Hemingway and Granville McDaniel (both on the far right). Billy Andrews is perched on the roof of the car.

No. C 6102.　　　　　The Bridge, City Island, N. Y. C.　　　　Hand Tinted.

This photograph of the City Island Bridge, with the City Island Bridge Park on the right, was taken in 1906. Notice the buildings in the background, many of which still exist. Horse car tracks lie along the bridge and on City Island Avenue.

This bird's-eye view of City Island Avenue with a horse car traveling north was taken c. 1900. The J.H. Rice Grocery Store, now the New Way Supermarket, sits at the corner of Fordham Street and City Island Avenue. Mr. Rice opened his store in the late 1800s and supplied residents with necessary supplies. Notice the Trinity Methodist Church steeple in the upper left.

City Island developed into a popular tourist attraction, with hundreds of visitors arriving each weekend. Although horse cars were the favored mode of transportation, some people walked to and from Bartow Station. This photograph, taken about 1908, shows the new steel bridge built in 1901. The new structure is situated in a more westerly direction from the old one connecting the mainland to Bridge Street.

The stagecoach transported people to and from City Island before the horse car line was introduced. The horse car line was owned by Judge Henry DeWitt Carey, a banker whose son, Harry Carey, became a famous Hollywood actor. Initially a one-horse operation, it left Belden Point and stopped at three locations on the island—Horton, Fordham, and Bridge Streets. People desiring to travel to New York City would then take the horse car to Bartow Station, pay a 5¢ fare to Westchester County, and board a trolley to 177th Street, where they would make another connection to the Battery.

The monorail failed as a mode of transportation. Complaints abounded, with passengers citing poor service, a lack of ventilation in the summer, and a lack of heat in winter. Sometimes the line would remain out of service for three days at a time. Cries of "get a horse" could always be heard. When the monorail broke down, people tried to find a livery car or walked to Bartow Station. The city discontinued the monorail in 1914 when the trolley arrived.

This interesting photo of the monorail and a horse car at the south side of the City Island Bridge was taken c. 1911. The lady in the street is the wife of Joseph Miller, the last village blacksmith on City Island. The young lady at the curb is Susan Miller. Mrs. Frapwell from Horton Street walks past Susan on the sidewalk. The man at the iron rail fence with the derby hat is Jim Feeley Jr.

Transportation rose to sophistication with the introduction of bus service in 1928 and with the growing number of people owning cars. Those considered affluent owned vehicles at the turn of the century. The above photograph, taken c. 1900, shows the Glasier and Smith families sitting in a typical vehicle of the era.

In 1931 the horse rail tracks were removed from City Island Avenue by the Works Progress Administration (WPA) to clear the way for buses and cars. The avenue was then raised, graded, and paved. Kay Hoffman Weiss sits on the fender of her family's car in the early 1930s. Notice how the style of cars had changed from those at the turn of the century.

The ferry dock on Hart Island is still used by a ferry that transports New York City's indigent from the City Island dock on Fordham Street to Hart Island for burial at Potter's Field, a distance of three-quarters of a mile. Prisoners have been performing the burials under the supervision of the New York City Department of Correction since 1869.

Several headstones on Hart Island mark the site of Potter's Field. The Department of Charities and Correction purchased the 102-acre island in 1868 for $75,000 from the Hunter family. The price paid included wooden buildings erected by the federal government during the Civil War for barracks and hospitals. Potter's Field was created on Hart Island in 1869 as a place to bury the city's poor and unknown. Louisa Van Slyke, a 24-year-old orphan, was the first internment on April 20, 1869.

Since Potter's Field opened in 1869, an estimated one million people have been buried here. A scandal brought about major reforms in the method of burial at Potter's Field. When wealthy planter Nathanial French died in 1873 at Bellevue Hospital, his remains were buried in a trench containing over 600 bodies. His friends could not obtain his body, and complained to officials who, in 1874, adopted an ordinance and new regulations to keep track of internments.

Potter's Field co-existed with other government programs on Hart Island at different times, including a prison work camp, a detoxification unit, a mental health facility, a Nike missile base, and Phoenix House, a drug rehabilitation center. After the turn of the century, prisoners were sent to Hart Island to learn various occupations. The Dynamo Room, built in 1912 and still in existence, served as a machine shop for inmates.

The government built a Nike electronically guided missile base in 1954 on 10 acres of Hart Island. The base was one of more than a dozen at that time guarding New York from atomic attack. This image shows the top of an underground storage and elevator structure that, although abandoned, still remains. Two underground rooms, 60 by 62 feet, stored 36 missiles. The radar control base on nearby David's Island instructed the Nike to hit the enemy. Today, only prisoners on burial detail and correction department personnel are allowed on the island.

Four

BUSINESSES DEFINE CITY ISLAND

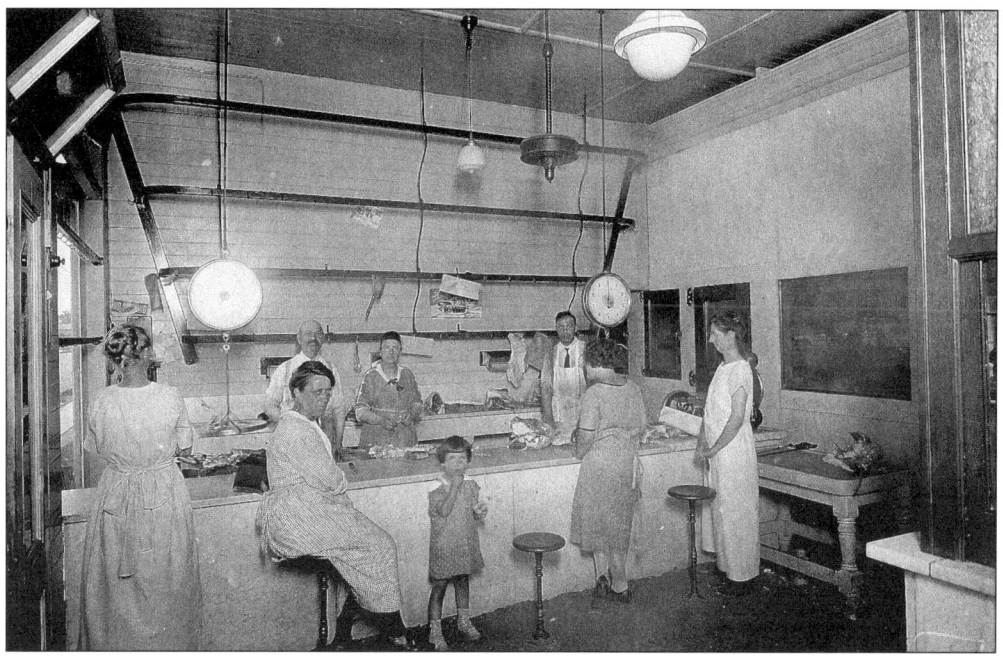

Charles Springer's butcher shop was located at 239 City Island Avenue, c. 1910. Trader John's marine store now occupies the site. Women traditionally purchased food products for the family in the early days. Several meat markets existed on the island before the turn of the century, including a meat delivery service three times a week in 1894 by Edward Cochran. Other butcher shops were S.F. Karlebach's Meat Market on City Island Avenue and Carroll Street; Booth's Meat Market at City Island Avenue and Schofield Streets, which opened in 1867; and J. Bender's Meat Market at the dock on east Carroll Street.

Charles Springer, his family, and workers pose at Springer's Butcher Shop, 239 City Island Avenue, at the corner of Carroll Street, *c.* 1920. Mr. Springer's father opened the butcher shop in 1904 and his son Charles (second from the right) operated the business until 1928. Charles and his father worked long hours in the store. In his early years, Charles participated in many City Island community activities. He was a member of the Royal Arcanum Lodge on the island, and played tuba in the City Island Band.

Springer's Market was located at 239 City Island Avenue, *c.* 1910. Charles Springer operated the business until 1928. He sold his City Island home on Schofield Street in 1964 to live in Florida, but visited the island every summer. He died in 1986 at the age of 98.

The J. Robson Marine Boat Supply store at 239 City Island Avenue, formerly Springer's Butcher Shop, is shown here c. 1930. Mr. Robson stayed at this location until the mid-1940s, when he moved to another site on west City Island Avenue, between Fordham and Bay Streets. Trader John's Marine Supply store is now located here.

Niedlich's Pharmacy at 530 City Island Avenue is shown here in the early 1900s. To the left of the picture stands Thwaites Shore House, which has since burned down. Captain Mike's Diving Service is now located at the site of the pharmacy. By the turn of the century, the island housed several drug stores, including Cook's Pharmacy at City Island Avenue and Hawkins Street and Reynolds Pharmacy on City Island Avenue near Fordham Street.

Samuel S. Miller's general store at 278 City Island Avenue became a popular place for men to purchase items and meet friends, c. 1908. Mr. Miller's family moved to City Island in 1869 and owned the business until 1910. The store featured foreign and domestic fresh and dried fruits, ice cream, soda water, cigars, and tobacco. Fireworks were sold here for July Fourth celebrations. Mr. Miller was a popular figure involved in the community. He founded the Military Band of the City Island Council, Royal Arcanum, and was president of the City Island Athletic Club.

Another view of Samuel S. Miller's general store at 278 City Island Avenue, 1910. From left to right are as follows: (seated) five unidentified men, John Burns, John Waterhouse, Grover Connelly, Charles Springer, Bert Ulmer, Adam Fennel, and two unidentified men; (standing) Roy Small, Sam Miller, Alfred Fordham, Eddie Horton, Bert Martin, Ernest Hemingway, Albert Garner, two unidentified men, Sam Merritt, George Baxter, and Sal Parlato.

The former Texaco Service Station on City Island Avenue, at the corner of Winter Street, is shown here *c.* 1940. The building remains a station and is currently owned by David Carman Jr., who has since renovated the property. This photograph was taken before the brick homes were built on Winter Street across from the station.

This is City Island Avenue looking north from Winter Street, *c.* 1935. Note the Sunoco Gas Station on the left and the Nevins Shipyard building on the right with many windows fronting the avenue. Further south, at east Centre Street near the present laundromat, a sandwich shop called Virginia's Luncheonette was a popular spot for young people in the 1940s.

By the time this c. late 1930s photograph was taken of City Island Avenue looking south near Fordham Street, many people owned cars, as evidenced by the vehicles parked along the avenue. The New Way Supermarket is now located on the right, and the City Island Donut Shop is across the street.

The old Dixon's Boat Livery and Tavern on Minneford Avenue, between Bridge and Terrace Streets, is shown here c. 1915. JP's Restaurant now occupies part of the building. Dixon's opened in the early 1900s as a canoe club. In later years, Dixon's sold food, bait, and offered mooring space for boats. The business closed about 1960 after the structure burned down.

This *c.* 1935 scene was photographed on City Island Avenue, looking south between Hawkins and Fordham Streets. The tailor shop later became the United Cigar Store. Rhodes Restaurant now occupies the building on the left.

George E. Hall's Hardware Store was located at the northwest corner of City Island Avenue and Fordham Street, *c.* 1910. Notice the building raised on blocks before the avenue was widened in the 1930s. After the hardware store closed, Samuel Bierman moved his pharmacy here from the opposite corner.

The City Island Diner, c. 1929–31, is shown here with owners Howard Cook (right) and George Cronk (middle). The owners employed island residents and operated the diner 24 hours a day until they closed the business in 1967. The structure still stands on its original cast-iron wheels on east City Island Avenue, between Fordham and Bay Streets. Horses originally transported the building from New Rochelle to City Island. Lazy Susan's Cafe now occupies the site.

Fritz's Cafe, originally operated by Charles Hill, was located in this turn-of-the-century, three-story structure at 259 City Island Avenue, at the southwest corner of Carroll Street, c. 1910. In 1939 Pat Reville established the Club Tavern here. In 1948 the building was destroyed by fire, but it was soon replaced with a new one-story building, which became known to many islanders as their "home away from home." Mr. Reville was well liked by islanders. He was a generous man, and during hard times he often helped people by giving them jobs and loaning them money.

Fire destroyed the first Club Tavern (formerly Fritz's Cafe) in the winter of 1948. The Helstrom, Hecker, and McGee families lived above the tavern and were successfully removed without serious injury. Owner Pat Reville rebuilt the tavern, which he operated until his death in 1984. The rebuilt structure was torn down in 1985, leaving an empty fenced-in lot at the corner of City Island Avenue and west Carroll Street. Notice the old Seafood Restaurant at the northwest corner of City Island Avenue and Carroll Street, now a modern structure housing a communication and design business.

This City Island meat market was located next to Fritz's Cafe on west City Island Avenue, off the corner of Carroll Street, *c.* 1910. A private house now stands on the site.

No. 24—City Island Avenue, looking North, City Island, N. Y.

City Island Avenue is shown here looking north, between Carroll Street and Hawkins Street, *c.* 1905. James D. Bell's Dry Goods Store on the left sold men and women's clothes and notions. Across the street are the sites of the former United Cigar Store and the City Island Arts Organization (CIAO) building.

Gerald Ford's house, 295 City Island Avenue, is decorated for Memorial Day, 1935. Mr. Ford operated a yacht brokerage business from the house and owned a 12-meter yacht named the *Nyella*.

Sam Bierman's Pharmacy was located next to the Ford House, at the southwest corner of City Island Avenue and Fordham Street, *c.* 1932. Mr. Bierman sold candy, film, and ice cream, and operated a Western Union service. Notice the penny weight scale outside the store. The building now accommodates the New Way Supermarket. Mr. Bierman later moved his pharmacy to the northwest corner of Fordham Street and City Island Avenue.

East City Island Avenue, between Fordham and Hawkins Streets, is shown here c. early 1940s. From left to right are a drug store, Nye and Miller's real estate and insurance office, Peerless Food Market, and a Chinese hand laundry. The laundry was owned by Jim and Eng King, the only Chinese family on City Island at that time. Islanders admired the King family, whose hard work and brilliant children were a credit to the community. Beginning in the 1880s, many businesses provided residents with basic necessities. Up until the mid-1930s, stores sold milk, eggs, meats, and fruits, and delivered their goods to residents of Tent City, Orchard Beach, located adjacent to the City Island Bridge.

These stores were located along east City Island Avenue across the street from the Ford House, between Fordham and Hawkins Streets, mid-1930s. Tom's Shoe Repair business can be seen on the left.

The Island Airways Flying School at the foot of east Fordham Street appears here in a *c.* 1948 aerial view. People could hire planes for sightseeing trips over New York and Long Island at the small seaplane base. City Island's Dr. Norbert Sander remembers that his first trip to City Island was at the age of nine, when he accompanied his father, who piloted a seaplane. The dock at the bottom leads to the ferry, which continues to carry the indigent and unknown to Hart Island for burial at Potter's Field.

Howard Smith worked at the Island Airways Seaplane Base at the foot of east Fordham Street when he was a youth in 1948. When the Airways became an accredited flight school, he was the first person to earn a pilot's license. A retired police sergeant, he has served as president of the City Island Civic Association for the last 12 years.

This winter scene at the Island Airways Flying School was photographed in 1948. Those holding a pilot's license could rent a seaplane at the base. When the Airways Seaplane Base and Flying School went out of business, a popular lounge known as The Airways operated until the 1960s. That business was eventually replaced by John Mini Indoor Landscapes.

This children's Halloween party took place at The Airways, located at the end of east Fordham Street, c. early 1950s. William McDaniel (left), manager Charles Mead (middle), and Kevin Cullen (right) are shown here. The tavern took over the site of the Airways Seaplane Base and Flying School.

Ursula Schliedermann (left), Charles Hanson (middle), and Evelyn Reutershan (right) pose in 1948 in Ursula's first ice cream parlor, located at the southeast corner of City Island Avenue and Fordham Street, the site of the City Island Diner and Donut Shop. Ursula and her husband, Ralph, later opened a donut shop further down the street, only to move again in the 1950s to 522 City Island Avenue, the current site of Fella's Lounge.

Howard Smith and Barbara Miller dance at Buckey's Tavern in 1948. Ms. Miller's family owned High Island and her father was an ambassador to Chile. The Drop Anchor Inn now occupies the site on City Island Avenue between Winter and Earley Streets.

The popular Raymond Theatre was located on City Island Avenue between Tier and Ditmars Streets, *c.* 1955. Built in the late 1920s by the Robinson family, the theatre originally boasted a front marquee. Benefits were held here during the Depression. Olin Stephens, the famous City Island shipbuilder, showed pictures of trans-Atlantic yacht races to raise money. In the late 1940s and 1950s, the theatre hosted beauty contests and talent shows. The City Island IGA Supermarket now occupies the site.

Entertainers perform in a stage show at the Raymond Theatre sponsored by the American Legion Hawkins Post, *c.* 1965. The theatre closed in the mid-1950s but reopened when James Russo and actor Sam Locante assumed ownership. They renamed it the City Island Theatre, installed a snack bar, and decorated the interior with antiques and old movie posters. The first documented theatre on City Island, known as the Leviness Theatre, was located at 103–105 Carroll Street, now a multi-family home.

Five

THE MARITIME CENTER OF NEW YORK

A reproduction of the *America* is shown here in 1968 at the Consolidated Yacht Yard in City Island. The original schooner won the first America's Cup trophy in 1851, after easily defeating 14 other boats in that memorable race around the Isle of Wight. The Cup, which acquired its name from the *America*, was successfully defended by the United States for 132 years until 1983. During that period, such internationally renowned people as Sir Thomas Lipton and Cornelius and Harold Vanderbilt commissioned shipyards on City Island to build yachts to defend America's Cup.

This is the 131-foot *Columbia*, dry docked in 1908 at Hawkins Shipyard, located on King Avenue and Fordham Street. The *Columbia* defended America's Cup in 1899 and again in 1901, skippered by City Island resident Charles Barr. The America's Cup race is the oldest continuous symbol of international sports competition and is the most sought after trophy in sailboat racing. Hawkins Yard, which serviced and stored the ship, was also where it was ultimately broken up.

The Benjamin F. Wood Boatyard, shown here c. 1920, was initially established on east Fordham Street. Mr. Wood moved the business to west Pilot Street before settling on a location at the foot of east Marine Street in 1921. Triboro Industries Marine Services later occupied the site; when Triboro closed down, the city approved a 57-unit condominium development for the area that has yet to materialize.

Henry B. Nevins' boat shed and office was situated on City Island Avenue, *c.* 1935. Public School 175 and its playground now occupy the site. Mr. Nevins played a significant role in shipbuilding in the United States—every 12-meter racing sloop built in the U.S., except for one, was built at Nevins Yard. The company built over 700 yachts, not including dinghies, small boats, and scores of 6-meter vessels. Mr. Nevins designed and built the first 24 YMS minesweepers in the country.

Henry B. Nevins (far right), boat designer Henry J. Gielow (center), and Holger Struckman (left), owner of the yacht *Nirvana*, pose in 1922. Mr. Nevins built palatial yachts for the wealthy using the finest materials and craftsmen. He purchased the property from Adam Hansen in 1906, who had acquired the yard from the City Island Athletic Club in 1902. Mr. Nevins helped many workers through hard times and financial troubles. He won a personal loyalty that carried over to the yard and the work it turned out.

The launching of the *Stormy Weather* took place in 1934 at Nevins Shipyard. This cruising yawl, designed by Olin Stephens, belonged to Philip Le Boutilier, who owned several department stores. Stephens' designs contained concepts that greatly influenced American cruising and racing boats. City Island yards shifted operations when the era of great yachts came to a close after World War II, building smaller, less-expensive boats.

Nevins Shipyard built new spars for the yacht *Windjammer*. Men are shown here transporting the spars in the mid-1930s, ready for installation on the yacht. The spars lie on top of a transporter in front of the Nevins Yard on City Island Avenue. During World Wars I and II, the government commissioned the City Island yards with their wide sheds and heavy hauling gear to build war vessels. City Island turned out minesweepers, torpedo boats, tugboats, sub chasers, landing craft, and freighters. Beautiful yachts were painted gray so they could perform patrol duty.

This photograph of the Nevins Piers was taken in the mid-1930s, when Long Island Sound turned to ice. The now-demolished piers were situated behind Public School 175, where the Nevins shed and office building once stood. Fire wiped out the yard in 1910, but Mr. Nevins borrowed money and rebuilt a new shop. Nevins turned out over 700 yachts, not counting hundreds of dinghies and small boats. His company was internationally known for building only the finest custom boats made to order—never stock boats.

Famous sailmakers Ratsy and Lapthorn Ltd., shown here in the early 1900s, began in England in 1796. The company came to City Island and established a sailmaking business in 1900 along the waterfront of Jacob's Boatyard at east Pilot Street. It then moved to Schofield Street next to Nevins Shipyard. A boatel condominium development known as The Sailmaker now occupies the site.

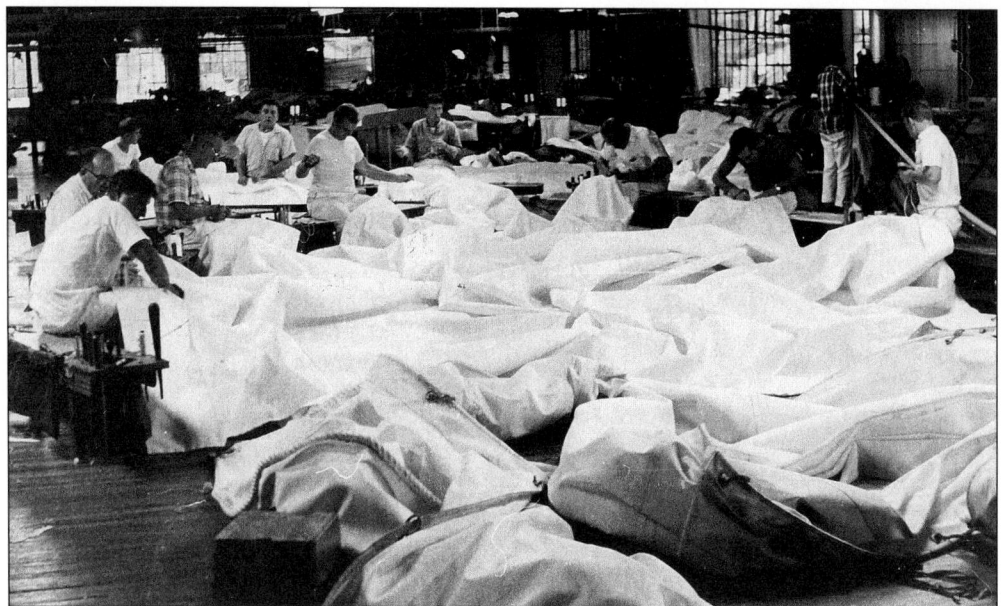

Workers are busy sewing sails by hand for the *Te Vega* at Ratsy and Lapthorn Sailmakers, *c.* 1950s. The world famous firm made sails for notable racing yachts, including America's Cup defenders. Ratsy's was responsible for two of the most striking innovations in the industry—the parachute spinnaker and the frostbite dinghy. Workers had to pass a four-year apprenticeship before they were considered professional sailmakers.

The Ratsy and Lapthorn building is on the far left in this 1903 photograph of Robert Jacobs' Shipyard, and the 146-foot-long *Reliance*, owned by a syndicate headed by Cornelius Vanderbilt and William Rockefeller, is on the right. The yacht won the America's Cup Trophy in 1903, and was the largest sailboat in the history of the America's Cup race at that time. Robert Jacob Sr. built 296 yachts while in business. Customers included Henry Ford, Luther Kellogg, Thomas Slocum, Vincent Astor, Peter Rouss, and Frank M. Smith, the Borax King.

Nevin's workers in 1929 transport a 158-foot hollow mast along City Island Avenue from Nevins Shipyard to Robert Jacobs' Shipyard, for installation on the yacht *Vanitie*. The *Vanitie* was out for the America's Cup contender, and had her sails made at Ratsy and Lapthorn. Owned by Gerard Lambert, she was a familiar sight around City Island for many years.

The 167-foot *Seven Seas*, the only full rig yacht in the country, sits at Robert Jacob's Shipyard on east Pilot Street in 1936. All other yachts were either schooners, ketches, or sloops. The exciting history of the Jacob's site begins with David Carll, who operated City Island's first boatyard here in 1835. Carll built the 146-foot *Ambassadress*, the largest schooner built in the U.S. at that time, for William B. Astor. Henry Piepgras purchased the yard in 1886 and sold it to Robert Jacob Sr. in 1900. The Consolidated Yacht Yard now operates at the site.

This view of Eastchester Bay behind Jack's Bait and Tackle on Cross Street and City Island Avenue was taken in the early 1940s. Notice the absence of marina slips at that time. Marinas gradually opened on City Island to accommodate the more popular smaller vessels.

The Minneford Yacht Yard, shown here *c.* 1955, is still operating at 150 City Island Avenue, which Henry Sayers purchased in 1926 and named after Native Americans who once lived here. Minneford built racing boats to defend America's Cup, many of which won the Cup trophy or other races—the *Dorade, Independence, Constellation, Intrepid, Intrepid II, Courageous, Freedom,* and the tenth *Enterprise.* In 1946, Phil Gauss became vice president and general manager of the yard.

The Minneford Yacht Yard built several of the first fiberglass boats made in the United States. This photograph, taken at the Minneford Yard in 1959, shows 34-foot-long fiberglass Trapper excursion boats. The yard also built several tugs and a riverboat made of fiberglass. During World War II, pleasure yachting on luxurious ships came to a halt, so Minneford and other City Island shipyards landed government contracts to build vessels for the Army and Navy.

This 1903 photograph shows the skeleton of a large vessel (name unknown) that had burned to the water line. It was towed to Sugar Loaf Beach, the site of the Minneford Yacht Yard. Notice the ship's plumbing and twisted debris. Pell Place is at the left of the picture.

An unexpected northeast storm hit City Island in December 1992, causing destruction and havoc, especially on the northeast side of the island. This photograph shows damage looking west on the north shore from JP's Restaurant.

Victor Anderson's dock, with John Stewart as dockmaster, is shown here in the late 1930s. Mr. Stewart told his family a story about actor Errol Flynn, who came to a City Island shipyard to commission the building of his yacht, getting into a brawl with a bar patron at the Paradise Inn, a tavern once located at the end of east Carroll Street.

This photograph of the American Car and Foundry Service Station (ACF) was taken from Anderson's Dock in 1931. The ACF was located between Anderson's and the Lyon Tuttle Shipyard at the southeast end of Fordham Street. The firm serviced the boats it sold in a large shed located on the property. The ACF remained in business, selling and servicing boats, from 1928 through the late 1930s.

Frederick Schmahl's gasoline barge *Esso* was photographed in 1926. Large yachts and steamers unable to dock at shore had to depend on these barges to deliver gasoline, coal, ice, water, and other goods through the 1940s. Today, gas and water docks on City Island provide these services. Schmahl's barge was 260 feet long and 30 feet wide. It berthed on the east side of City Island Avenue off Pilot Street. Smaller boats, which eventually replaced palatial yachts, docked at fast-growing marinas to obtain supplies.

Steve Jensen enjoys a sail around City Island in the early 1950s. High Island, a summer bungalow colony near City Island, and the High Island Bridge lie in the background. Smaller vessels became the rage after World War II. Eventually, the invention of fiberglass decreased the demand for wood boats. Vessels were now built elsewhere in fiberglass factories. City Island took to servicing pleasure boats as well as catering to boat owners in the form of marinas, restaurants, nautical shops, etc. Businesses sell bait and tackle, rent fishing boats, feature sailing lessons, and offer memberships to boating clubs.

Olin Stephens, in his 90s, poses at the 1998 City Island Maritime Festival. He is the dean of yacht designers, with more outstanding yachts to his credit than anyone over the past 70 years. In 1928 he formed the team of Sparkman and Stephens, locating offices across the street from Nevins Shipyard. He designed several America's Cup winners, including the *Freedom 12*, *Columbia*, *Constellation*, *Intrepid*, and *Courageous*. Working with the Nevins, Minneford, Jacob, and Kretzer Yards, he designed and built scores of famous boats.

Six

A FASHIONABLE ERA

The Belden Point Inn was a popular dining and dancing spot at Belden Point and City Island Avenue, c. 1920. Visitors to the island at that time sought high-toned bistros and restaurants, and during Prohibition the wealthy considered City Island quite fashionable. Music and dancing at the inn were provided by Dinty Moore's Belden Point Inn Orchestra. The inn's specialty was steamed clams. A shore dinner ran $2.50, while a duck dinner was $2. Both entrees were reduced to $1.25 on Sunday afternoons and weekday evenings.

Maxim Beach and Pavilion, a popular bathing resort, operated at the foot of east Fordham Street near Hawkins Shipyard, c. 1920. The pavilion featured food, swimming, and entertainment. Grand places such as the Soundview Hotel at the foot of west Carroll Street, the Bayview Hotel at Bridge Street, Bracker's Restaurant at Pell Street and City Island Avenue, and the L'Aiglon Restaurant (now the Lobster Box) attracted tourists to City Island.

Thwaites Bayshore Restaurant and Hotel was located at the corner of City Island Avenue and Cross Street at the turn of the century. Established in 1870, Thwaites Restaurant and Hotel was later known as Thwaites Restaurant. The building was destroyed by fire in 1992, leaving a fenced-in empty lot. In its heyday, Thwaites evolved into one of the finest restaurant and dancing establishments in the area. Sleighing parties came to Thwaites from as far away as Tremont Avenue and Mt. Vernon to enjoy a good time.

The East Shore Pavilion at the foot of east Ditmars Street is shown here *c*. 1910. The pavilion was originally named the Macedonia Hotel and Inn after the British ship *Macedonia*, which was captured by the United States in the War of 1812. The inscription on the building describes the legend. The ship's timbers were allegedly used to build the hotel, but further research reveals that they were the remains of another vessel of the same name. The hotel, also known as Casino Beach and Crescent Beach in the 1920s and 1930s, featured boating, bathing, and dining.

The Harlem Yacht Club, located on Hunter Avenue on the western shore of City Island, is shown here *c*. 1900, several years before it was destroyed by fire in 1915. Members built a new building in 1939 at the same site. The club was organized in 1883 and originally started out as a model sailboat club at 123rd Street and the Harlem River. Members eventually purchased their own regular sailboats and decided to establish a clubhouse on City Island. The Harlem Yacht Club remains one of four yacht clubs on City Island.

No. 172. Belden Point   City Island, N Y

April 2nd Birthday Greetings from Mrs. D. J. Summer

This is a *c.* 1900 photograph of the Morris Yacht Club at Belden Point. Shortly after William Belden purchased Stephen D. Horton's property and house in 1885, he sold it to Collis P. Huntington, the Central Pacific Railway magnet. Mr. Huntington willed the property to Columbia University, which leased it to a syndicate in 1914, whose grandiose plans of creating a European resort failed. The club originally occupied the Bowne House at Rodman's Neck, but the building was destroyed by fire in 1904.

The Morris Yacht Club is shown here *c.* 1915. The Huntington Mansion became the Monte Carlo Hotel, and by 1917 was known as the Chateau Laurier, a popular dancing and dining spot. In 1925, Lou Gold and other famous bandleaders entertained here. A copy of the January 6, 1917 menu advertised broiled salmon steak for 60¢ and filet mignon for $1. The offices of the City Island Athletic Club were housed here before the Morris Yacht Club purchased the property in 1937.

84

This rare photograph of the City Island Yacht Club when it was a private home at the end of west Pilot Street was taken in the early 1900s. The Kirchofs, who owned the house, used it as a summer residence. Arthur Kirchof was the recording secretary of the club for most of his life. Formed in 1905 at Herman Cordes' boatyard on Cross Street and incorporated in 1907, the club moved several times on City Island.

Members of the City Island Yacht Club finally settled their clubhouse in the 1920s at its present location on west Pilot Street. They acquired their first clubhouse in 1910, a two-story building on west Cross Street. The club moved again in 1913 to the east side of Cross Street, then in 1919 for a short time to the southwest side of Pilot.

Stuyvesant Yacht Club members have a good time at Tent City, Orchard Beach, where their clubhouse was located in 1918. The clubhouse, with its spacious grounds, stood near Jack's Rock at Orchard Beach.

Stuyvesant Yacht Club members enjoy a New Year's Eve party at the clubhouse at the foot of Centre Street, c. 1939. This building burned in 1968 but was rebuilt the following year. The club was established in 1889 when members purchased the dismantled ferry *Gerard Stuyvesant* and towed it to the Port Morris creek in the Bronx. The club incorporated in 1890, several years after renting a store in Manhattan.

Commodore Gustave A. Gallowitz Sr. congratulates his son, Gustave A. Gallowitz Jr., on his recent election as commodore of the Stuyvesant Yacht Club in 1965. The younger Gallowitz, in becoming commodore at the age of 37, repeated an honor that was his father's in 1925 at the same age. Gallowitz Sr., who purchased the present clubhouse site on Centre Street in 1935, died in 1974, having been a club member for 60 years. He purchased the property on City Island after Parks Commissioner Robert Moses decided to tear down tents at Orchard Beach and build a formal beach. Stuyvesant members had to leave their spacious grounds at Orchard Beach, which had boasted two marine railways and a fleet of over 100 boats.

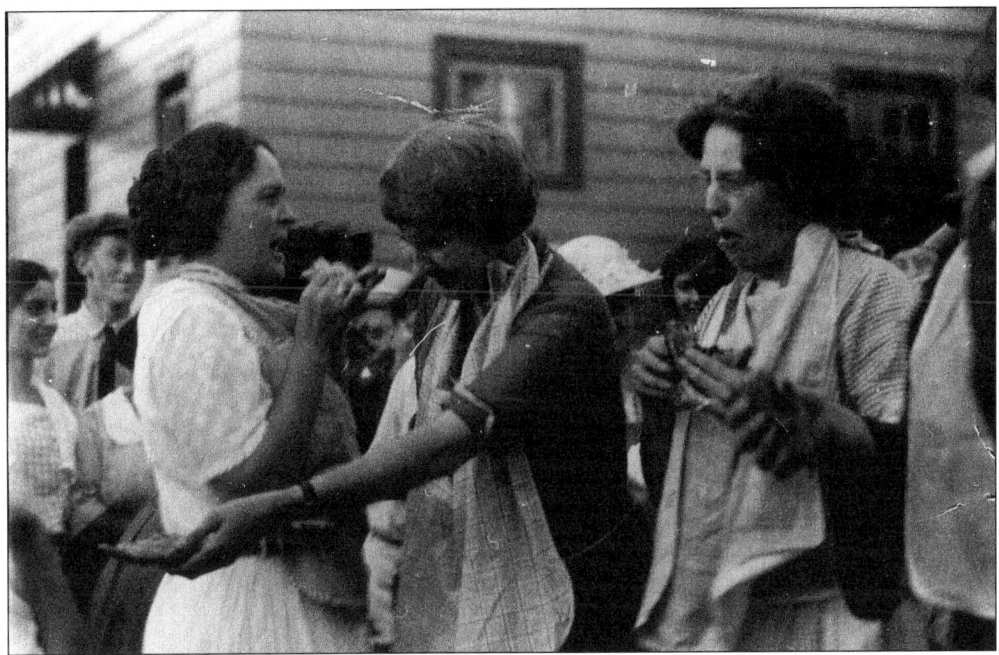

Stuyvesant Yacht Club members enjoyed many leisure times. This photograph shows members competing in a pie-eating contest at the club's headquarters at Tent City in Orchard Beach, *c.* 1920s. In 1904, when the club rented a house in Port Morris, members became involved in one of the greatest disasters of maritime history. They rescued 110 passengers from the excursion boat *General Slocum*, which caught fire as it passed Hellgate in the East River, causing the death of 1,021 passengers.

On Delmour's Point, the point of land jutting out into Eastchester Bay along the western shoreline of City Island, sits a large Victorian home at the end of Tier Street. Shown here in 1908, the property was once owned by politician Larry Delmour and continues as a private residence. *Long Days Journey Into Night*, with actress Katharine Hepburn, was filmed in 1962 at this turn-of-the-century mansion.

The old Colonial Inn, formerly the Marshall House, lay adjacent to the City Island Bridge on the side of Pelham Bay Park, Orchard Beach. Attorney Elisha W. King built this Greek Revival mansion about 1829. He named the house Hawkswood and used it as his country seat. Levin P. Marshall later purchased the property. Despite the fact that the city government initially determined the house should be preserved and turned into a museum, the building was demolished in the early 1930s.

Seven

TENT CITY, ORCHARD BEACH

No. 18—Camping at Pelham Bay Park, N Y.

By the time this turn-of-the-century photograph was taken, vandalism had forced the New York City Department of Parks to limit the use of nearby Hunter and Twin Islands, and a burgeoning tent community had arisen on parkland at the northeast side of the City Island Bridge. Parks charged a minimal seasonal fee for a campsite. Permit holders initially erected temporary bungalows of canvas, but these later evolved into permanent structures. In 1934 the city government gave campers one year to remove their bungalows, after which work began on building the new Orchard Beach.

Permit holders built tents on permanent wooden platforms on the average 30-by-60-foot site. Tents were constructed with a 3-foot wood section, topped by framed screens, over which canvas was drawn and supported by a ridge pole across a peaked roof. The canvas sides could be lowered or raised by means of stakes, according to the weather. Residents were required to dismantle their camps at season's end, leaving only the plank floor. The other components, including furniture, were stored in small bathhouses. A typical tent is shown here about 1910.

Tent City sprouted into a mini-metropolis. Streets were named alphabetically with their own associations quickly developing. The baker, milk man, butcher, ice man, and other tradesman came at least once a day. Even the mail man made regular deliveries. The parks department removed garbage daily, and the *Bronx Home News* was delivered to over 200 subscribing families.

Tent City was separated from nearby Rodman's Neck Naval Station by only a thin wire fence. This wire separated 10,000 servicemen from the summer dwellers during World War I. When young sailors drilled, they were cheered on by the campers, who rushed out with buckets of cold lemonade and jelly water for their refreshment.

Tent City was the scene of great social activity. The area buzzed with athletic events and games in which everyone participated. B Street, a grassy area 100 feet wide by 400 feet long, was used for games such as sack races, tugs of war, and croquet. Lawn parties were held here under the light of 300 Chinese lanterns. Plenty of food and beverages were available, and local talent provided entertainment.

Near the camp a large wooden pavilion provided a spot for a dance floor. Volunteer pianists or a wind-up phonograph supplied the music. On Saturday evenings a small dance band entertained the campers. Girls sometimes performed recitals or danced in chorus lines.

Adults engaged in many forms of entertainment and organized their own clubs, such as the "C Street Jolly Women's Club" and the "B Street Horseshoe Club." These two men were clowning around for the camera in 1924. Many tents were considered beautifully decorated, and their occupants were embued with outstanding community spirit. American flags and Chinese lanterns swung from most structures. Each tent was numbered and some had names like "Spare Time" and "Idle Four." Iceboxes and oil stoves were kept inside, separated by a dividing curtain. Residents drew water from taps installed on nearby pipes. Young adults walked over the City Island Bridge for shore dinners, or danced at City Island's many hotels and nightclubs.

Children figured out their own pastimes with little parental supervision. Youngsters are shown here digging for clams for dinner. Hunting four-leaf clovers, examining insects, toasting marshmellows and potatoes, flying kites, playing tag and hide and seek—all of these filled a child's day. Youngsters helped adults keep tents neat and well arranged in hopes of winning an award for the nicest tent. Young and old alike maintained two fire pails at the tent—one filled with water, and another with sand. Records of 1908 show that approximately 1,500 people lived here from June to September. By 1926 the number had grown to 3,500. The parks department reports that in 1919 the complex featured 1,548 lockers and 126 dressing booths with showers.

A family enjoys summer's cooling breezes and lazy moments in 1915. Swimwear at the time was markedly different from today's fashions. Families began renewing camp permits for up to 20 years for fees ranging from $10 to $30. As seasons passed, the tents sprouted wooden sides, metal screening, front and back porches, and gardens.

By 1927, many permit holders wired their tents for electric lights, built cement or brick walkways and steps, installed telephones, and constructed private boathouses. Permanent types of furniture, such as the wooden rocking chair next to Adele Tingo Henshaw (far left), found its way into the tents. The bathhouses doubled as furniture storage areas during the winter. In fact, people could now occupy the structures all winter for an additional $10 fee!

Adele Tingo holds a neighbor's baby at the campsite in 1921. The Tingo family's tent was located next to Mrs. Patton, who hosted the Orchard Euchre Club meetings at her tent every other week. Euchre was a popular American card game, and the club was one of many clubs formed among campers to pass the evenings together. Sadly, this good life slowly came to an end in the late 1920s. New York City residents began to look at the area with skepticism. Permit holders made up rules and regulations to keep outsiders from using the beaches, and it seemed only political favorites could obtain permits. By the early 1920s, campsites became real estate holdings, selling for over $1,000, with permits reverting to the new owners.

Labor Day climaxed the season with a great ceremony raising the American flag on a large flagpole. The entire area was decorated with American flags to commemorate the important event. Throughout the day, everyone at the camp participated in races and games. That night, a party with music, dancing, eating, and drinking marked the end of summer.

People enjoy the refreshing Long Island Sound waters at Tent City in Orchard Beach, c. 1930. Bathhouses provided showers, toilets, and changing rooms. By the early 1920s, up to 600 vehicles parked on weekends and holidays along the unused portion of Tent City facing Long Island Sound.

Typical tents at Orchard Beach began selling for over $1,000 on public property. Farsighted city residents wanted to reclaim the parkland for the public as a refuge for poor families, and as a place to bring children for outdoor play.

Campers organized their own street-cleaning, fire-fighting, and life-saving corps. This is a rare picture of the Tent City, Orchard Beach Life Saving Station. During the storm of June 11, 1921, the *Bronx Home News* reported that Ed Otto, in charge of the Orchard Beach Station, rescued 15 people from overturned boats and brought in one dead.

Rowboats, the popular means of transportation at Tent City, were used to travel to City Island for shore dinners and other entertainment. A changing era began in 1927, when the City Island Improvement Association, represented by James J. Tobin, brought a lawsuit against Bronx Parks Commissioner Joseph P. Hennessy and his policy of issuing permits. The suit claimed that the colony had evolved into a permanent private settlement on public parkland.

Campers enjoy water sports at Tent City in 1932, several years after a reprieve. When Mr. Tobin and City Islanders succeeded in temporarily enjoining all permits, the politicians immediately took over. The Appellate Division modified the previous decision, allowing campers to stay for the summer of 1927. Mayor Jimmy Walker later signed a bill officially declaring the tent colony legal. Tent City operated until 1934, when plans for a new Orchard Beach were announced.

When New York City Mayor Fiorella LaGuardia appointed Robert Moses as the parks commissioner, work began in earnest to remove the tent structures and create a beach known as the "Riviera of New York City." This photograph shows a section of landfill in the form a crescent-shaped beach. City Island and City Island Bridge are visible in the background. It took four years (1934–38) and 3 million cubic yards of sand and fill to fully complete the new Orchard Beach.

This aerial view of Orchard Beach was taken in the summer of 1938. The fill and sand operation connected Hunter Island (upper right) to the parking lot. The work ultimately attached Orchard Beach to Rodman's Neck on the park side of the City Island Bridge. In 1947 the one-mile beach was lengthened by half a mile to include Twin Island, which up to that time remained separated by a small inlet. The beach could hold approximately 200,000 people and 7,000 cars.

This aerial view of Orchard Beach was taken in 1938. The new recreation area featured a large bathhouse complex, restaurants, a dance area, terraces, ball courts, locker rooms, comfort stations with showers, police and first-aid facilities, and a playground. Firework displays decorated the sky every Wednesday evening during the summer.

The bathhouse plaza mall is shown here in 1938. The fountain on the right lasted until the 1950s. City Island can be seen in far background. The mall, 1,400 feet long and 250 feet wide, showcased elm trees and exotically designed flower beds. To protect the quality of life at the beach, policemen issued many tickets for infractions such as picking flowers, walking on the grass, littering, and dressing scantily. Taking pictures at the beach was illegal in 1942 under wartime regulations.

Thousands of people flocked to the beach on opening weekend in 1938, clogging roads with cars and buses. City Island residents complained about the massive undertaking, which caused traffic jams and the loss of business on City Island. City government responded by widening the Shore Road leading to the beach and creating other paved access roads. Despite roadway improvements, traffic presently remains congested during the summer months.

This view of Twin Island from Hunter Island was taken looking due east in 1931. Hunter and Twin Islands became popular as camping, picnicking, and swimming areas beginning in the late 1800s. The islands lay adjacent to Tent City, Orchard Beach, and were connected to the mainland when the city built the new Orchard Beach. Twin Island consists of two land masses known as East Twin (right) and West Twin (left). The city demolished the former mansion on East Twin in 1937.

The Twin Island house is pictured here at the turn of the century. Twin and Hunter Islands became part of Pelham Bay Park in 1888, when New York City began acquiring land for park development. The house was known as the Fish Mansion, Ogden Mansion, and Hoyt House, depending on who lived there at the time. The city demolished the structure in 1937 because it could not maintain the property.

The parks department leased the Twin Island House beginning in the early 1900s to the Jacob Riis Foundation for a children's summer retreat. Approximately 86 underprivileged youths lived here each summer and participated in recreational activities under the Riis Settlement House Program.

The women in this *c.* 1904 photograph were involved with the Jacob Riis Foundation at Twin Island. Prior to 1911, people traveled to Twin Island by boat or canoe. When the city built a concrete-reinforced pedestrian bridge connecting Twin to Hunter Islands, people could walk here. They crossed over a causeway situated along the Shore Road, entered Hunter Island, and then used the pedestrian walkway between the two islands.

A group of campers who paddled to Twin Island from the Throggs Neck area of the Bronx sit in the Twin Island house, *c.* 1920. The city government issued camping permits to various organizations for sites on Twin and Hunter Islands. In 1914 the Working Girls' Association maintained two tents on Twin Island. Parks supplied running water to the camp after discovering that the existing well water was polluted. Members of the DeLasalle Institute regularly surveyed the Twin Island coastline.

A grand two-story Georgian-style mansion loomed atop the highest point at the central section of Hunter Island. Built in 1812 by island owner John Hunter, the house showcased paintings by Rembrandt, Rubens, and Titian. When the city purchased Hunter Island as part of Pelham Bay Park in 1888, it leased the house to welfare organizations for $1 a year. Members of the Society of Little Mothers pose in front of the house in 1905.

A motorboat is being used to tow canoes from Hunter Island back to Throggs Neck after a day outing in 1916. When the government established a naval base at nearby Rodman's Neck, the parks department in 1918 temporarily discontinued issuing recreation permits for Twin and Hunter Islands, citing security reasons.

A large group of youths canoed to Hunter Island in 1919 to barbeque and swim. To protect the environmental refuges of Hunter and Twin Islands, New York City Mayor John V. Lindsay signed the Hunter Island Marine and Geology Sanctuaries Bill on October 11, 1967, curtailing all activities that threaten the wildlife, grasses, and woodlands of both islands.

Young people enjoy a summer day on Hunter Island in 1919. The number of visitors to Twin and Hunter Islands surged as transportation to the area improved. Sunseekers arrived by trolley lines or walked from the nearby Bartow Train Station. Littering and fire problems began to escalate, forcing the parks department to curtail recreational activities on both islands.

This view of the Hunter Island Inn was taken from the Shore Road in the early 1900s. A.E. MacLean served as its proprietor for many years. The inn stood along the Shore Road opposite the gateway to Hunter Island. The property and mansion formerly belonged to Elizabeth DeLancey, a daughter of Elias Hunter, a descendant of John Hunter.

Tony and Olga DeAngelo arrive at their summer bungalow on High Island with sons Al (left) and Tony (right). An upscale bungalow colony existed here from the early 1900s to 1959. This privately owned 4.3-acre island lies a half mile off the northeast coast of City Island. A footbridge at the end of Terrace Street on City Island connects High Island to City Island. When Tony was 9 years of age, he rowed daily to City Island, purchased milk, and sold the milk to High Island residents. Youths spent their extra money on treats at the Nickel Palace on City Island near the bridge.

The Sola and DeAngelo families maintained a summer residence on High Island, *c.* 1927. All families were forced to leave in 1959, when Nan Miller sold the property to NBC and CBS to erect a broadcasting transmitting tower. Families who leased property from Ms. Miller tried unsuccessfully to raise $100,000 to purchase the property. Before the High Island footbridge was built in 1928, people either rowed from High Island to City Island, or walked across a sand bar at low tide.

Albert Sola built a lifeguard station on High Island that also served as his family's summer home. Mr. Sola volunteered his services as a lifeguard for the bungalow community. The house, shown here *c.* 1930, featured various amenities, including a brick fireplace. People who were handy came together to build wood bungalows and a 40-foot boardwalk.

A group of High Island residents pose for the camera in 1924. The group includes Al Sola (sitting on the right) and members of the Walsh and Reilly families. Approximately 37 families lived on High Island during the summer season. A caretaker lodge was the only structure on the island before it turned into a bungalow colony. In the early 1900s, Nora and Jack Beatty worked as the island's caretakers and were allowed to rent out sites for a summer camp.

High Island's lifeguards pose in 1928 with Nan Miller (in the back wearing a hat), who owned High Island from 1928 to 1959. In 1762 High Island was owned by Captain John Wooley. Ownership passed to Elisha King from 1829 to 1872. King Avenue on City Island is named for Elisha, who purchased shoreline property on City Island opposite High Island to secure a landing easement to and from High Island.

High Island residents found many ways to entertain themselves. In 1927, a group of children dressed in costumes prepare to put on a show, one of the island's gala events. Fishing excursions and dances were popular pastimes. High Island youths played baseball games against the City Island Civic Association team. Promising members of the High Island team included Billy Italiano, Hugh Black, Ed Loughman, Allen Henshaw, Carl Silvagni, and Gerry Knapp.

Summer revelers participate in a summer carnival at High Island in 1930. Note Al Sola's lifeguard house on the right. The summer complex began as a tent community, but by 1930 all tents were upgraded to wooden bungalows. Before the Miller family owned the property, the island was owned by David Curtiss of Mt. Vernon, and the Midtown Club in Manhattan.

Eight
THE COMMUNITY SPIRIT

The City Island Football Team, shown here in 1908, was one of many sport teams sponsored by the City Island Athletic Club. Shown here are, from left to right, as follows: (front row) unidentified, Mr. Sadler, John Rolf, unidentified, and Curley Price; (middle row) Gus Barton and two unidentified men; (back row) Sam Reynolds, three unidentified men, Harry Carey, three more unidentified men, and Nelson McClellon. The City Island Athletic Club, incorporated in 1900, rose as a major force in sponsoring sports teams and activities. The club operated an arena at Belden Point in the early 1930s where it held boxing bouts, tennis tournaments, and baseball games.

The Marion Cadets, a cornet band, was formed in 1895. Shown here in 1908, it was sponsored by Samuel Miller and named in honor of his daughter. From left to right are as follows: (front row) John Bowle, Bob Vickery, unidentified, Ben Barstow, Ned Booth, two unidentified men, and Willie Winkleman; (middle row) Mr. Paine, two unidentified men, Sam Reynolds, John Rolf, and Bill Booth; (back row) two unidentified men, Orrin Fordham, unidentified, and Dr. Lawrence. Mr. Miller also founded a military band that entertained at various sites.

Cub Scout Pack 211 poses for a picture in the Trinity Methodist Church, c. 1950. City Island has a long history of forming competitive sports groups and other organizations. Before 1935, groups such as the Minneford Basketball Club, the City Island Wheelman, the City Island Shipyard Bowling League, and the Non-Pareil Baseball Club existed. Jafsie Condon, the man who won notoriety in the Charles Lindbergh baby kidnapping case of 1932, was manager and captain of the City Island Baseball Club in 1906.

Troop 211 Scouts and their den mothers pose in the late 1970s at the Grace Episcopal Church. Scouting provides youths with life skills and acceptable social behavior.

The Civic Day parade took place each year on City Island Avenue in the early years. This photograph shows Scouts and other City Island organization members marching past Rochelle Street in the late 1940s. Notice the former Fishermen's Wharf on the left.

The Pelham Masonic Lodge, shown here *c.* early 1930s (prior to renovations), is located at the corner of City Island Avenue and Schofield Street, opposite Robson's Boat Supplies (now Trader John's). The lodge was organized in 1871 with 12 members who met over a small carpenter shop on City Island Avenue. John O. Fordham presided as the first master. The lodge raises money for various causes and remains involved in charitable activities.

By the turn of the century, membership in the Masonic Lodge grew, but its finances were compromised due to a fire in the building they were renting. Fund-raising events were held to buy property and construct a building. With 302 members, the lodge purchased two lots in 1926 at its present location. Members pose here for a picture after a *c.* 1930s meeting.

The annual City Island Board of Trade dinner took place at City Island's Ryans Restaurant in 1936. The board of trade began on City Island in the late 1890s and is the forerunner of the City Island Chamber of Commerce. Samuel Bierman, president of the board of trade for many years, also received the Brotherhood Award from the City Island Civic Association. Peter LaScala currently serves as president of the City Island Chamber of Commerce.

City Island youths socialize and enjoy a sunny winter day after a snowfall at the corner of Fordham Street and City Island Avenue, c. 1930s.

City Island Navy men pose in front of Cooks Diner in 1946 after World War II. They are, from left to right, as follows: (kneeling) Howard Smith and Robert Dorsey; (standing) "Boop" Garrett, Bob Dallesandro (middle, dressed in white), and an unidentified man. Cooks Diner is now the newly renovated Lazy Susan's Cafe on City Island Avenue, between Fordham Street and Bay Street.

Frequent family gatherings on City Island were common in the early days. Pictured on City Island in 1941 are the following, from left to right: (front row) Bart DeStefano, Ena Persteins Ellwanger, and Ann DeStefano; (back row) Aida Scolarici and her mother, Aida Scolarici, Mrs. Paino, Alice Persteins, Catherine DeStefano, and Joseph DeStefano.

Members of the Leonard H. Hawkins American Legion Post 156 pose c. 1948. Island residents were proud of their patriotism, conducting parades and celebrations honoring those in the service. All the men in the picture served in World War II. The Hawkins Post was organized in 1919 and named in honor of one of City Island's war heroes, who is buried in the cemetery on King Avenue.

The Hawkins Post American Legion's bazaar at Vidal Marina's parking lot is shown here in August 1947. Members raised money to buy their own building through various benefits. In 1951, the legion purchased its current site at the corner of Cross Street and City Island Avenue. Vidal Marina is now the Royal Marina. In the early days, post members rented a room for their meetings at Brown's Hotel on Fordham Street and Brown's Lane. They also rented space in a handkerchief factory located on east Bay Street.

Singers Joan White (left) and William Clancy perform in a minstrel show at the new City Island Theatre in the 1960s. Shows put on by the American Legion at the former Raymond's Theatre (now the IGA Supermarket) was one way of funding various projects.

Officers of the Hawkins Post American Legion pose for a photograph in 1994. From left to right, they are as follows: (sitting) Joe Goonan, Doug Malin, William Clancy, Bill Treanor, and Vincent Hecker; (standing) Buddy Scollon, John Foley, Bob Booth, John Ulmer, Tom Heffernan, Edward Shipp, Donald Varian, Joe Goulden, and Benjamin Kelly. The post organized the Ladies Auxiliary and Sons of the American Legion, whose members are involved in many activities. It sponsors field days, clambakes for veterans, and cancer benefits. Members also maintain veterans' graves at the City Island Pelham Cemetery.

Members of the Leonard Hawkins Post honor veterans each Memorial Day. This picture was taken in City Island's Pelham Cemetery in 1993, one of City Island's oldest landmarks. In 1881 the cemetery on King Avenue was incorporated as the Pelham Cemetery Association. The first burial site on City Island was located at 190 Fordham Street, where the old school building now stands. Remains were transferred to the new cemetery to make room for the school. Many of the community's founding members are buried here.

The American Legion Hawkins Post leads the country in fighting for the release of prisoners of war and finding those missing in action. William Clancy is currently the New York State Chairman of the Prisoners of War Committee. This photograph was taken at a Memorial Day parade in the early 1990s.

The City Island Little League remains one of the most popular sports teams for boys and girls on City Island. Before the City Island Little League Field was built adjacent to Public School 175, youths played at ballfields in Rodman's Neck. This photograph was taken *c.* 1978.

The island came together in 1976 to celebrate the country's bicentennial. Participants worked hard creating floats and costumes for the parade, and sponsored a grand Bicentennial Costume Ball.

The 1976 Bicentennial Parade was something to watch. The City Island Volunteer Ambulance Corps (ambulance on left) began on City Island in 1972, after a delay in the city's Emergency Medical Services ambulance caused the death of a young man. The Ambulance Corps ceased operating in 1990 because fewer and fewer people were willing to devote time for medical training and staffing the ambulance.

Vintage cars show off at City Island's 1976 Bicentennial Parade. This photograph was taken on City Island Avenue near the corner of Pilot Street. The Grace Episcopal Church can be seen in the upper right.

Art fairs along City Island Avenue delight residents and visitors each year. Both photographs show people enjoying an afternoon at the fair in 1975. The City Island Arts Organization (at 278 City Island Avenue) and the City Island Chamber of Commerce sponsor the event, which features music and activities for children. Many artists and craftspeople who live on City Island welcome opportunities to display their products. Businesses such as Focal Point Gallery, Starving Artists, Down by the Sea, and Corona's Hidden Treasures successfully accommodate artists.

Members and guests of the Garden Club of City Island are shown here at the club's annual luncheon in 1993. Pictured in front is Susan Strazzera. The others are, from left to right, Marilyn Sinclair, Jill Weber, Helen Reel, Margaret Conway, The Rev. Dolores Henderson, Parks Department Commissioner James Ryan, and Jennie Varian. The Garden Club, founded in 1960, is a member of the Federated Garden Clubs of New York State. It has won awards for various flower displays and operates a street clean-up program. Jackie Kyle Kall, a local realtor, was the first club president.

Virginia Gallagher (left) and Sr. James Patrick were photographed in 1998 at New York City Mayor Rudolph Giuliani's inauguration ceremony. Ms. Gallagher is the managing agent of Pilot Cove Manor senior residence on east Pilot Street. A community activist for many years, she is a member of Community Board 10 and former president of the City Island Historical Society and Community Centre. Sr. James Patrick has served as principal of St. Mary Star of the Sea School since 1985.

This chile tasting contest took place at Rhodes Restaurant in 1993. Kneeling on the left is Tyler Rhodes, owner of the restaurant. City Island cafes and restaurants periodically sponsor events for the community. The Black Whale Inn and Laura's Cafe regularly feature poetry readings and art exhibits.

Members and friends of the west Fordham Street Beach Association gather for a day of swimming, eating, and games, c. 1990s. The association property boasts bathrooms, showers, a picnic area, and a kitchen.

The City Island Chamber of Commerce honors various members of the community in recognition of their activism and civic work. Chamber President Peter LaScala (far left) in 1996 gave Sara S. McPherson (with microphone) the Tom Cerreta Accomplished Business and Service Award. Since 1974, Ms. McPherson worked as managing editor of the *Island Current*, City Island's local newspaper. Ena P. Ellwanger (far right) received the Exemplary Community Service Award. Ms. Ellwanger, principal of Public School 175, is noted for her devotion to students and excellent administrative skills.

Residents and guests enjoy lazy social times on boats at the many marinas on City Island. People either stay on their boats at the marina docks, or take their vessels out for a cruise.

Both photos show islanders and visitors enjoying a weekend of folk singing and art at the City Island Arts and Crafts Fair, *c.* 1993. The Humpty Dumpty bounce game (at bottom) entertains youths. The fair is sponsored by the City Island Chamber of Commerce and the City Island Arts Organization (CIAO).

The first annual Fleet Weekend and Maritime Festival held in June 1998 proved a great success. It was a glorious celebration of the community's past and present. Hundreds of visitors, residents, politicians, and students participated in a wide variety of activities under sunny skies. The gala event was sponsored by the City Island Chamber of Commerce, IDEA (Innovative Directions, an Educational Alliance), and the City Island Nautical Museum.

The 92-year-old schooner *Mary E.*, owned by former City Island resident Teddy Charles, returned to City Island for the Fleet Weekend and Maritime Festival in June 1998. The *Mary E.* was docked at Consolidated and Sagman's Shipyard on City Island from 1973 to 1991.

City Island scouts pose for a picture at the Minneford Dock during the Fleet Weekend and Maritime Festival in June 1998. Events included sails on classic wooden yachts, folklore chats, sailing races, a moonlight cruise, an arts and crafts festival, a shark program by the North Wind Museum on City Island, breakfast at Fordham Street beach, breakfast at LeRefuge Bed and Breakfast, a fishing contest, chowder tasting, programs at the Nautical Museum, Sea Shanty music, and concerts by Irish-American bands. The weekend ended with a dinner affair at the Morris Yacht Club.

Classic yachts came to the Maritime Festival in 1998 and docked at the North Minneford Yacht Club behind Public School 175. The *Sirius* (pictured above) was designed by Olin Stephens and built in Nevins Shipyard, the current site of the public school. Mr. Stephens, over 90 years old at the time, traveled to the festival from New England. Another schooner, the *Golden Eye*, built at Minneford Shipyard in 1937, also arrived at the event to participate in the festivities.

126

City Island youths celebrate the record-breaking 1998 World Champion New York Yankees team. Tyler Rhodes put together the letter painting for this picture.

The City Island Arts Organization (CIAO) holds its annual art auction at the Morris Yacht Club in November 1998. Residents and CIAO members look forward to this yearly event as it offers interesting works of art, food, and lots of fun.

This photograph shows several members of the City Island Community Center and James Vacca (right), district manager of Community Board 10, City of New York. From left to right are Peter LaScala, Tom Smith, Deirdre Simmons, and Mr. Vacca. The Community Center is housed at the old Public School 17 building on Fordham Street along with the Nautical Museum and 16 condominium units. The center offers adults and youths an opportunity to participate in various classes, and offers rooms for meetings and entertainment. Mr. Vacca was instrumental in working with the city government to save a portion of the building for community use.

Members of the City Island Historical Society pose in front of their museum headquarters at 190 Fordham Street, the site of the former Public School 17. They are, from left to right, as follows: (front row) Joyce Maloney, Virginia Gallagher, and Joyce Gleason; (middle row) Jay Sinclair, Barbara Dolensek, Carol Stewart (standing behind Ms. Dolensek), Fil Magavero, and Edward Sadler; (back row) Jorge Santiago, President Skippy Lane, Helen Reel, Dr. Fred Hess, Russell Schaller, Maury DeCandido, and Tom Nye. Chartered in 1975, the historical society features special and permanent exhibits at the museum, and works with schoolchildren teaching them City Island history.